Jill Rowley on #SocialSelling

140 Tweets on Modern Selling the Social Way

By Jill Rowley

A Starter Kit for Social Selling

E-mail: info@thinkaha.com
20660 Stevens Creek Blvd., Suite 210
Cupertino, CA 95014

Published by THiNKaha®
20660 Stevens Creek Blvd., Suite 210, Cupertino, CA 95014
http://thinkaha.com

First Printing: October 2014
Paperback ISBN: 978-1-61699-136-4 (1-61699-136-4)
eBook ISBN: 978-1-61699-137-1 (1-61699-137-2)
Place of Publication: Silicon Valley, California, USA
Paperback Library of Congress Number: 2014953617

Trademarks

Warning and Disclaimer

Acknowledgments

I'd like to applaud all those who are blazing the #SocialSelling trails with me. Keep connecting, sharing, and engaging. #BeHuman

Why I Wrote This Book

#SocialSelling is a new concept that requires evangelism. It's a mindset shift from SELLING to SERVING and HELPING. It's a new skillset and it requires an enabling toolkit. My purpose is to enrich other people's careers and elevate the profession of sales. I love to learn and teach (in under 140 characters at a time). You are what you tweet.

Jill Rowley

Twitter: @jill_rowley

Website: www.jillrowley.com

Email: jill@jillrowley.com

LinkedIn: www.linkedin.com/in/jillrowley

How to Read a THiNKaha® Book
A Note from the Publisher

The THiNKaha series is the CliffsNotes of the 21st century. The value of these books is that they are contextual in nature. Although the actual words won't change, their meaning will change every time you read one as your context will change. Experience your own "aha!" moments ("ahas") with a THiNKaha book; ahas are looked at as "actionable" moments—think of a specific project you're working on, an event, a sales deal, a personal issue, etc. and see how the ahas in this book can inspire your own ahas, something that you can specifically act on. Here's how to read one of these books and have it work for you.

1. Read a THiNKaha book (these slim and handy books should only take about 15–20 minutes of your time!) and write down one to three actionable items you thought of while reading it. Each journal-style THiNKaha book is equipped with space for you to write down your notes and thoughts underneath each aha.

2. Mark your calendar to re-read this book again in 30 days.

3. Repeat step #1 and write down one to three more ahas that grab you this time. I guarantee that they will be different than the first time. BTW: this is also a great time to reflect on the actions taken from the last set of ahas you wrote down.

After reading a THiNKaha book, writing down your ahas, re-reading it, and writing down more ahas, you'll begin to see how these books contextually apply to you. THiNKaha books advocate for continuous, lifelong learning. They will help you transform your ahas into actionable items with tangible results until you no longer have to say "aha!" to these moments—they'll become part of your daily practice as you continue to grow and learn.

As Thought Leader Architect & CEO of THiNKaha, I definitely practice what I preach. I read *#POSITIVITY at WORK tweet, #MANAGING YOUR VIRTUAL BOSS tweet*, and one new book once a month and take away two to three different action items from each of them every time. Please e-mail me your ahas today!

Mitchell Levy
publisher@thinkaha.com

Contents

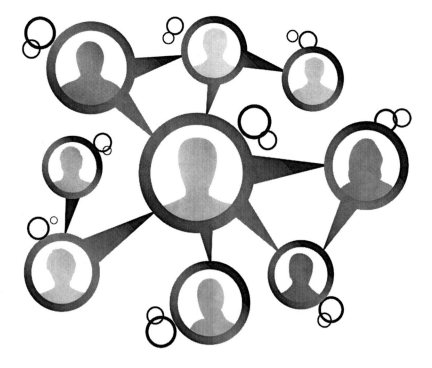

Section 1
What Is #SocialSelling and Why Should You Care?

Your sales force is on the brink of EXTINCTION. They're being replaced by search engines and social networks—it's time to adapt and evolve or be replaced. B2B buyers are anywhere between 57 percent to 70 percent through the buying process prior to engaging with sales. Your buyers are having learning parties without you. Meet the Modern Buyer: she's digitally driven, socially connected, mobile, and empowered with unlimited access to information and people. Is your sales team prepared? Simply put, #SocialSelling is using social networks like LinkedIn and Twitter to do research to be relevant to build relationships that drive revenue.

1

#SocialSelling is using social networks
to do research to be relevant to build
relationships that drive revenue.
@jill_rowley

_____

_____

_____

2

All selling is social. Always has been.
Always will be. #SocialSelling @jill_rowley

_____

_____

_____

3

#SocialSelling is technology-enabled research, networking, and relationship-building. @jill_rowley

_____

_____

_____

4

As a business or person, #Social isn't something you do—it's something you are. #SocialSelling @jill_rowley

_____

_____

_____

5

#SocialSelling starts with a mindset shift from Selling to Serving. Buying behavior has changed; so should the way we sell. @jill_rowley

_____

_____

_____

6

The path to social business is actualized by the social employee. #SocialSelling @jill_rowley

_____

_____

_____

7

Social networks connect you with people, not faceless targets or records in a database. #SocialSelling @jill_rowley

_____

_____

_____

8

#SocialListening can lead to conversations. Sales reps should be listening for buying signals. #SocialSelling @jill_rowley

_____

_____

_____

9

If you're going to be active in #Social, don't just RT or shamelessly plug your brand! #SocialSelling @jill_rowley

_____

_____

_____

10

You are what you eat (strikethrough) tweet.
#SocialSelling @jill_rowley

11

92% of #B2B buyers start their search on the
Web. #SocialSelling @jill_rowley

12

Social media is making it easier to network and build relationships. The Web never sleeps and knows no geographic boundaries. @jill_rowley

---

13

#SocialSelling doesn't change the fundamentals; it enhances good salespeople. @jill_rowley

---

14

#SocialSelling is recognizing that the
buying process is controlled by a better
informed and more connected customer.
@jill_rowley

_____

_____

_____

15

Without realizing tangible revenue from social activity, it's just a waste of time and effort. #SocialSelling @jill_rowley

_____

_____

_____

16

The modern buyer is digitally driven, socially connected, mobile, and empowered. It's time to embrace #SocialSelling. @jill_rowley

_____

_____

_____

17

Social networks improve the results of skilled salespeople, leveraging a sound sales process. #SocialSelling @jill_rowley

_____

_____

_____

18

Getting started with #SocialSelling is easy. Business cards are LinkedIn connections and new people to follow on twitter. @jill_rowley

_____

_____

_____

19

Content is the currency of the modern sales professional. Use content to earn trust. #SocialSelling @jill_rowley

_____

_____

_____

20

Jill Rowley's purpose is to enrich other people's careers and elevate the profession of sales. #SocialSelling @jill_rowley

_____

_____

_____

21

Social media could quickly become
anti-social for those doing #SocialShouting.
#SocialSelling @jill_rowley.

_____

_____

_____

22

Ppl don't like to be sold. They like to buy.
Help them buy the way they want to buy,
which may not be the way you want to sell.
@jill_rowley

_____

_____

_____

23

Are you a #socialselling leader or lagger? Use LinkedIn's social selling index to see how you rank. http://www.slideshare.net/linkedin-sales-solutions/social-selling-index-measure-your-social-selling-and-drive-more-pipeline @jill_rowley

_____

_____

_____

24

#SocialSelling Index leaders (http://www.
slideshare.net/linkedin-sales-solutions/
social-selling-index-measure-your-social-
selling-and-drive-more-pipeline) create 45%
more opportunities than SSI laggers.
@jill_rowley

_____

_____

_____

25

#SocialSelling Index leaders (http://www.slideshare.net/linkedin-sales-solutions/social-selling-index-measure-your-social-selling-and-drive-more-pipeline) are 51% more likely to hit quota than SSI laggers. @jill_rowley

_____

_____

_____

26

The future requires your employees to understand and engage with social for your business to thrive. #SocialSelling @jill_rowley

_____

_____

_____

Section II
How to Get Started with #SocialSelling

So, how do you "do" #SocialSelling? Move from using LinkedIn as your online resume, to managing your digital reputation—optimize your profile for the buyer, not the recruiter. Your network is your net worth, so ABC—Always Be Connecting. Socially surround the buyer, the buying committee, and their sphere of influence. Read what your buyers read and share that content across your social networks. Use social networks to listen to what's happening in your buyers' world. As with all sales strategies and tactics, don't expect results and profit right away. Gaining influence and engaging with future advocates takes time and you have to nurture relationships. The results will soon be tangible as people begin to trust you, your business, and what you have to say. Use these tips to get the best value out of #SocialSelling.

27

Getting started with #SocialSelling?
Evangelize the Why, Define the What,
Enable the How. #SocialSelling @jill_rowley

_____

_____

_____

_____

28

Read what your buyers read and share
that content across your social networks.
#SocialSelling @jill_rowley

_____

_____

_____

29

Leverage your personal connections on
social networks for warm introductions.
#SocialSelling @jill_rowley

_____

_____

_____

30

The first step in becoming a #SocialSeller is
to build your personal brand. @jill_rowley

_____

_____

_____

31

You should utilize your social channels for lead prospecting. #SocialSelling @jill_rowley

---

32

Achieving real results takes much more than just gleaning your social networks and mass blasting. #SocialSelling @jill_rowley

_____

_____

_____

33

Attend events virtually by following the event hashtag, attendees & speakers. Engage in the Twitter conversation. @jill_rowley

_____

_____

_____

34

Try to figure out how to best leverage your existing social networks in order to identify and nurture leads. #SocialSelling @jill_rowley

_____

_____

_____

35

The biggest challenge is how to get everybody out of their comfort zones. #SocialSelling @jill_rowley

_____

_____

_____

36

Make your first interaction more impactful by writing an engaging, personalized message. @jill_rowley

_____

_____

_____

37

Power to the people! Buyer-to-company trust is 33%, buyer-to-buyer trust is 92%. #SocialSelling @jill_rowley

---

38

Encourage your current advocates to engage your future advocates http://bit.ly/t-l-b-p. #SocialSelling @jill_rowley

---

39

Sales reps are closing bad deals; you should make sure that your customers are the right fit for the value you can deliver. @jill_rowley

---

40

Lead with data. Follow with passion and emotion. #SocialSelling @jill_rowley

---

41

Use social media to earn trust & to build relationships. #SocialSelling @jill_rowley

_____

_____

_____

42

Successful #SocialSellers optimize their social profiles for the buyer, not the recruiter. @jill_rowley

---

43

#SocialSelling has redefined ABC "Always Be Closing" to "Always Be Connecting." @jill_rowley

---

44

Social research helps you find the buyers, the buying committees, and their sphere of influence. #SocialSelling @jill_rowley

---

45

You can be an insider in your decision makers' network by being active on social media. #SocialSelling @jill_rowley

---

46

There's always a way to follow up with someone. #SocialSelling gives you another channel to connect with your buyer.
@jill_rowley

_____

_____

_____

47

Listen to the problems your buyer has. Engage by adding insight and value, not by selling. #SocialSelling @jill_rowley

_____

_____

_____

48

I'm down with OPC (Other People's Content), yeah you know me. Share 3rd party, thought leadership content. #SocialSelling @jill_rowley

_____

_____

_____

49

Reference others online who support your product or POV, particularly if it's a trending topic. #SocialSelling @jill_rowley

_____

_____

_____

50

Be active in the social conversations your customers are having. #SocialSelling @jill_rowley

_____

_____

_____

51

Ignite a sense of excitement and a sense of urgency with your future advocates. People want to be inspired. #SocialSelling @jill_rowley

_____

_____

_____

52

Kick your #SocialSelling into high gear with a little help from Marketing. #ContentIsCurrency @jill_rowley

_____

_____

_____

53

If you suck offline, you're going to suck more online. #Don'tSuck #SocialSelling @jill_rowley

---

54

With social sales intelligence, you can reach buyers at exactly the right moment. #SocialSelling @jill_rowley

---

55

#SocialSelling begins and ends with
listening. @jill_rowley

_____

_____

_____

56

Be in the right place at the right time in
social when a sales opportunity presents
itself. #SocialSelling @jill_rowley

_____

_____

_____

Section III
Do's and Don'ts of #SocialSelling

Although there aren't any set rules to #SocialSelling, there are general do's and don'ts that make up the realm of social etiquette. You will sell more when you serve and help more. Don't use social networks as a new channel for SPAM. These are some tips that I've learned throughout the years.

57

Know what #SocialSelling is and what it isn't. It isn't modern trickery. @jill_rowley

_____

_____

_____

58

#SocialSelling success isn't just about popularity metrics, it's ultimately about building pipeline and driving revenue. @jill_rowley

_____

_____

_____

59

Set goals for audience, content, and engagement. Set business goals that you can track. #SocialSelling @jill_rowley

_____

_____

_____

60

Be your authentic self. Respond to customers. Post at least once a day, but not too often. #SocialSelling @jill_rowley

_____

_____

_____

61

Make sure your content caters to your audience. #BeRelevant #SocialSelling @jill_rowley

_____

_____

_____

62

You wouldn't ignore your customers' phone calls or emails, so don't ignore them on social. #SocialSelling @jill_rowley

_____

_____

_____

63

Experiment and innovate ways to expand your social presence. #SocialSelling @jill_rowley

_____

_____

_____

64

Integrate social networking into your everyday routine & into your traditional sales channels & processes. #SocialSelling @jill_rowley

_____

_____

_____

65

Email signatures and business cards are great places to start promoting your social accounts! #SocialSelling @jill_rowley

_____

_____

_____

66

Know the importance of setting goals and
hitting your numbers. Social can help you.
#SocialSelling @jill_rowley

_____

_____

_____

67

Don't think you can just randomly participate on social media and see positive business results. #SocialSelling @jill_rowley

_____

_____

_____

68

Don't risk losing friends by flooding their
feeds with irrelevant and annoying content.
#SocialSelling @jill_rowley

_____

_____

_____

69

Make sure to strike a balance between diversity and frequency of posts. #SocialSelling @jill_rowley

---

70

Social is two-way, not one-way. #EngagementIsNotOptional. #SocialSelling @jill_rowley

---

71

Use social media as an opportunity to demonstrate your professionalism and accessibility. #SocialSelling @jill_rowley

_____

_____

_____

72

Don't expect to see incredible results on your first day or week. #SocialSelling @jill_rowley

_____

_____

_____

73

Aim for clear and achievable goals so that your social networking efforts don't go to waste. #SocialSelling @jill_rowley

_____

_____

_____

74

Monitor what your competitors are saying, so you can spot competitive movement & opportunity to react earlier. #SocialSelling @jill_rowley

_____

_____

_____

75

Hitting your sales number is not just about working harder. It's about smarter #BuyerCentric selling. #SocialSelling @jill_rowley

---

76

Go social to deepen your relationships with your customers. #SocialSelling @jill_rowley

---

77

Be a trusted advisor. Try to add value and build trust within your buying community. #SocialSelling @jill_rowley

_____

_____

_____

78

Do research. Combine social monitoring and intelligence to know what interests your buyers. #SocialSelling @jill_rowley

---

79

Be authentic. It's a big deal in social. Violators of this rule are unwelcome. #SocialSelling @jill_rowley

---

80

Don't be fake or sneaky. Users rule social,
and will do everything to create a
non-spammy place to engage.
#SocialSelling @jill_rowley

_____

_____

_____

81

Nurture your customers, partners, and
future advocates. Social networks allow you
to stay top of mind. #SocialSelling
@jill_rowley

_____

_____

_____

82

Don't talk about yourself all the time. To be interesting, be interested. #SocialSelling @jill_rowley

_____

_____

_____

83

Don't push products. Being pitchy is unwelcome. #NarcissistsNotWelcome #SocialSelling @jill_rowley

_____

_____

_____

84

Don't bombard leads. Don't immediately message them on every platform, begging to give a demo or to visit your site.
@jill_rowley

_____

_____

_____

85

Relationships take time to develop.
No one gets married on the first date.
#SocialSelling @jill_rowley

_____

_____

_____

86

Don't be nasty. Share how you can help others succeed. #Give2Give. #SocialSelling @jill_rowley

_____

_____

_____

87

Talk about and share other's content—not just yours. #OPC #SocialSelling @jill_rowley

_____

_____

_____

88

You can't be a trusted advisor if you can't hold a conversation without pitching. #SocialSelling @jill_rowley

_____

_____

_____

89

Constantly bragging about yourself or your company is a turn off. #SocialSlut #SocialSelling @jill_rowley

_____

_____

_____

90

Incorporate social into your day. It
should be a part of your daily activity.
#SocialSelling @jill_rowley

_____

_____

_____

91

Set aside time to research, curate, and share content. #SocialSelling @jill_rowley

_____

_____

_____

92

Use social for knowledge. Understand what others may be interested in, their likes and interests. #SocialSelling @jill_rowley

_____

_____

_____

93

Be where your buyers are offline at events and online in social networks. Be there #AllTheTime. #SocialSelling @jill_rowley

_____

_____

_____

94

Build quality relationships. Join groups, add comments to blog posts, and feel free to join conversations. #SocialSelling @jill_rowley

_____

_____

_____

95

Avoid being a robot. Take time to leave personalized comments. #SocialSelling @jill_rowley

_____

_____

_____

96

Familiarize yourself with the social
courtesies of each network. Use
common sense. Don't do #SocialStupid.
#SocialSelling @jill_rowley

_____

_____

_____

97

Use good judgment when following up with others. #SocialSelling @jill_rowley

_____

_____

_____

98

Don't just post anything.
Make a plan to share a range of content.
http://ahaamplifier.com #SocialSelling
@jill_rowley

_____

_____

_____

99

#NeverGiveUp Building a social presence takes time. #SocialSelling @jill_rowley

_____

_____

_____

Section IV
How Does #SocialSelling Affect People?

In the vast world of social media, it's easy just to say something quickly and send it out into the world without thinking twice about it. When you start #SocialSelling, however, you don't want your messages to get lost in the sea of tweets, retweets, likes, favorites, shares, etc. A good way to go about it is to think of your social networks as tight-knit communities to which you can contribute. Share content that would be interesting and relevant to the community. Engage with OPC (Other People's Content). First and foremost, be honest, transparent, and human.

100

Social media is confusing, chaotic, crowded, noisy & unfiltered. The wild, wild west of the World Wide Web. #SocialSelling @jill_rowley

---

101

Social networks reveal a person's identity and their relationships, making sense of social media. #SocialSelling @jill_rowley

_____

_____

_____

102

Use social networks to find, listen, relate, connect, engage, and amplify buyers and their sphere of influence. @jill_rowley

_____

_____

_____

103

Share honest and direct customer stories with your future advocates at the beginning of the buying cycle. #SocialSelling @jill_rowley

_____

_____

_____

104

There has to be a level of trust, not only between the sales team and marketing, but the salesperson and the buyer. @jill_rowley

_____

_____

_____

105

Step 1 to modern B2B demand generation is realizing that your future advocates don't care about your company. #SocialSelling @jill_rowley

_____

_____

_____

106

Always be helping. Be human.
#SocialSelling @jill_rowley

107

#SocialSelling success journey: mindset
shift, new skillset, and enabling toolkit.
@jill_rowley

108

Your best salespeople are your customer advocates; figure out how to amplify their advocacy. #SocialSelling @jill_rowley

---

109

Engaging with millennials requires empowering them to be part of the solution. #SocialSelling @jill_rowley

---

110

People will forget what you said, and forget what you did. But people will never forget how you made them feel. #SocialSelling @jill_rowley

_____

_____

_____

111

70% of buying experiences are based on how the customer "feels" they are being treated. #SocialSelling @jill_rowley

_____

_____

_____

112

Act appropriately. Treat buyers as people, not as transactions. #SocialSelling @jill_rowley

---

113

The social employee humanizes the brand. #SocialSelling @jill_rowley

---

114

People do business with people they know,
like & trust. #SocialSelling @jill_rowley

_____

_____

_____

115

Your success correlates to the level of authenticity you demonstrate throughout the process. #SocialSelling @jill_rowley

_____

_____

_____

116

An individual should understand goals, strategy, objectives, and tactics in the age of social. #SocialSelling @jill_rowley

_____

_____

_____

117

Speak out quietly, because quiet is often
better than yelling. #SocialSelling
@jill_rowley

_____

_____

_____

118

To be interesting, you need to be interested
in something other than yourself.
#SocialSelling @jill_rowley

_____

_____

_____

119

Everyone deserves to bring all of who they are to work, to be their authentic self. #SocialSelling @jill_rowley

_____

_____

_____

120

Greatness is a matter of conscious choice and discipline, not circumstance. #SocialSelling @jill_rowley

_____

_____

_____

121

Brand advocates are 50% more influential than the average customer. #SocialSelling @jill_rowley

_____

_____

_____

122

I eat failure for breakfast so I can dine on success for dinner. @jill_rowley

_____

_____

_____

123

Your Network is Your Net Worth.
@PorterGale nails it in her book.
#SocialSelling @jill_rowley

_____

_____

_____

124

We're living in the Age of the Customer.
Companies must be #CustomerCentered
#CustomerCentric #CustomerObsessed.
@jill_rowley

_____

_____

_____

125

LinkedIn is not just a place to find your dream job, but a way to be better at the job you already have. @jeffweiner #SocialSelling

_____

_____

_____

126

Just as salespeople are moving into the future, buyers are already ahead of us. @kokasexton #SocialSelling

_____

_____

_____

127

Sales needs to learn more abt Marketing;
Marketing needs 2 learn more abt Sales.
We all need 2 learn more abt our
CUSTOMERS! @jill_rowley

_____

_____

_____

Section V
Encouragement

It's hard to get started with #SocialSelling and to make it a daily habit. Here are some words of encouragement to get you on your way! Beliefs lead to behaviors. #UCanDoIt.

128

Admit when you have messed up and do what is necessary to make it right. Respect people's boundaries. #ShitHappens @jill_rowley

_____

_____

_____

129

The cheaper you are when it comes to investing in a professional sales force, the worse your results will be. #SocialSelling @jill_rowley

_____

_____

_____

130

Doing something differently takes
learning something new. #SocialSelling
@jill_rowley

_____

_____

_____

131

It's easier to sell to someone who
has already purchased from you.
#TurnYourCustomersIntoAdvocates
#SocialSelling @jill_rowley

_____

_____

_____

132

You should make extra efforts to connect
socially w/ the ppl who influence your
buyers. I use @GetLittleBird. #SocialSelling
@jill_rowley

_____

_____

_____

133

"You have to wake up with an attitude of gratitude." -Zig Ziglar #SocialSelling @jill_rowley

_____

_____

_____

134

Join some groups today, and add some tomorrow. #SocialSelling @jill_rowley

_____

_____

_____

135

Provide value, and demonstrate authentic
interest in your work. #SocialSelling
@jill_rowley

_____

_____

_____

136

Don't fall behind on the conventions of social media. Put yourself ahead of your competition. #SocialSelling @jill_rowley

---

137

Stop selling and start serving your buyer. #SocialSelling @jill_rowley

---

138

The power in selling today is not in what you know. It's in what you share. You are what you tweet. #SocialSelling @jill_rowley

_____

_____

_____

139

Don't give to get. Give to give!
#SocialSelling @jill_rowley

_____

_____

_____

140

I spent 52 quota-crushing quarters @Salesforce & @Eloqua. A year driving #SocialSelling @Oracle. Need help? I'm here! www.jillrowley.com

What Are Your Ahas?

Thanks for reading *Jill Rowley on #SocialSelling*!

Got any "Ahas" that would fit with this book?

We'd love for you to share them!

Tweet us **@thinkaha** and/or **@jill_rowley**, and tag your Ahas with **#SocialSelling**.

About the Author

Jill Rowley, one of the most dynamic voices on Social Selling and Modern Marketing, has developed programs to help B2B companies market, sell, and service the modern buyer. Jill was named the #1 Most Influential Woman in Social Selling via Forbes. She is a keynote speaker, workshop leader, and agent for change. Jill's expertise is at the nexus of marketing and sales, which can no longer operate as individual silos. Today's buyers are more knowledgeable than ever about their intended purchases. Jill is a #SocialSelling evangelist and #ModernMarketing expert. She provides strategy and planning, offers keynote speeches and workshops, and has developed curriculum to educate and enable sales professionals on the why, what, and how of social selling.

Prior to launching her own company, Jill was the Social Selling Evangelist and Enablement leader at Oracle, was the top revenue generating sales professional at Eloqua (known as the "EloQueen"), and a top performing Account Executive at Salesforce.com. Her work at Oracle included designing, deploying, and driving adoption of a global Social Selling program for Oracle's 23,000 sales professionals.

Jill's 2014 speaking experiences have included Cloud World in India, Business Marketing Association's Global Conference, Social Media Marketing World, a guest appearance on #SalesforceLIVE with 177k viewers, HubSpot's INBOUND conference, LinkedIn's Sales Connect event, Dell's #SocBiz Think Tank event in San Francisco, various keynote speeches for GE, keynote presentations to 1,700 Symantec sales and marketing professionals, and remote presentations to 3,500 Mitel employees and partners.

In the fall of 2014, Jill is scheduled to speak at Dell's UnConference in Austin, Salesforce.com's Dreamforce event, Draper University, Vidyard's Video Marketing Ignite conference, the TrackMaven Marketing Summit in New York, 2014 National Middle Market Summit, and numerous other client engagements for TD Ameritrade, Intuit, ASCO Numatics, Red Hat, CA Technologies, TIBCO, and Cornerstone OnDemand.

Books in the THiNKaha® Series

The THiNKaha book series is for thinking adults who lack the time or desire to read long books, but want to improve themselves with knowledge of the most up-to-date subjects. THiNKaha is a leader in timely, cutting-edge books and mobile applications from relevant experts that provide valuable information in a fun, Twitter-brief format for a fast-paced world.

They are available online at http://thinkaha.com or at other online and physical bookstores.

The Aha Amplifier helps you increase your influence by amplifying quality "Aha" moments! Each Aha is sharable via Twitter, LinkedIn, Facebook, and Google+, so you can easily share an important idea or statement with thousands (if not millions) of people.

Sign up for a free account at
http://www.AhaAmplifier.com today!

Please pick up a copy of this book in the Aha Amplifier and share each Aha socially at
http://bit.ly/JillRowley-AhaAmp01.

CPSIA information can be obtained
at www.ICGtesting.com
Printed in the USA
FSOW02n2213201214
4066FS

9 781616 991364